THE AUTHORITY OF SCRIPTURE IN A POSTMODERN AGE

SOME HELP FROM KARL BARTH

ROBERT D. CORNWALL

Topical Line Drives Series
Volume 9

Energion Publications
Gonzalez, Florida
2014

Cover Design: Henry Neufeld

ISBN10: 1-63199-005-5
ISBN13: 978-1-63199-005-2

Energion Publications
P. O. Box 841
Gonzalez, FL 32560

energionpubs.com
pubs@energion.com
850-525-3916

INTRODUCTION

The late twentieth century witnessed, so it is said, the demise of the modern age, which began three centuries earlier. This new Age of the Enlightenment that emerged in the late seventeenth century hailed the primacy of reason. One could and should understand the world by way of the senses and rational deduction. It was a blessing for the sciences, but it relegated God to the background. Truth was self-evident and did not depend on divine revelation.

Nowhere is this vision of reality better revealed than in this statement from the American Declaration of Independence.

> We hold these **truths to be self-evident**, that all men are created equal, that they are endowed by their Creator with certain unalienable Rights, that among these are Life, Liberty and the pursuit of Happiness.

Jefferson wrote, and his colleagues affirmed, that the idea that "all men are created equal" was self-evident. While we might affirm that premise, history demonstrates that it the identity of this "all men" wasn't all that self-evident after all. Obviously it didn't include women or persons of color. These persons didn't seem especially endowed with inalienable Rights such as "Life, Liberty and the pursuit of Happiness." Only with time and much struggle did the truth present in these words become truly self-evident. I might add that we're still in the process of trying to understand to whom these inalienable Rights apply.

With regard to the Bible, the Enlightenment mindset suggested that reason could discern the self-evident truths that are present in this sacred book. Many appealed to common sense. Remember, Billy Graham didn't say "this is how I read the Bible." No, according to Graham, it is "the Bible says." Scripture is clear; it's meaning being self-evident. My own faith community – the ecclesial descendants of the nineteenth century American religious reformers Alexander Campbell and Barton Stone – has long lived with similar assumptions. Many of my co-religionists have believed that all Christians need to do to understand God's truth is to read the Bible without the interference of external sources, such as creeds. Then they will reach agreement on the simple gospel facts. This will lead, my spiritual ancestors believed, to unity among Christians. This belief is rooted in a Modern/Enlightenment mindset that assumes that truth can be discerned through common sense.

Many contemporary forms of American Protestant Christianity have been influenced by this philosophy, especially modern evangelicalism. Looking back into the early nineteenth century we find a pioneering Protestantism that was quite practical and even rationalist in nature. Yes, there was enthusiasm and emotion as seen in the revivals on the frontier, but there also was a desire to cut through the clutter of inherited theologies and find a reasonable Christianity that made sense of the modern world. One of the resources that many turned to was the inductive science of Francis Bacon. To this was added the Enlightenment philosophies of John Locke and Scottish philosopher Thomas Reid. These philosophers provided the philosophical foundation for Alexander Campbell's religious enterprise, an enterprise founded on belief in the clarity and authority of the biblical text for all matters of religion.

In many ways the world benefited from the Enlightenment vision, but its appeal to simplicity didn't always make the best sense of the world around us. Many people had the sneaking suspicion that there is more to this world than what reason (including the sciences) could reveal. They began to wonder where God fit into this scheme. Where is the mystery? Efforts to align Christian faith with the Enlightenment left us with a faith that seemed static and shallow.

One response to this sense of concern was the idea that we have moved into a post-modern age. Postmodernism suggests that reality is more complex than the modernist vision. With regard to faith, some postmodernists suggested that perhaps there was room for mystery and complexity. When it came to the reading of Scripture, perhaps things aren't as clear and as self-evident as we thought. Maybe truth and fact are not always one and the same.

As the sciences rose to prominence over the past three centuries, providing answers to questions that seemed in conflict with traditional religion, religious authority, including biblical authority, became suspect. While Campbell and his evangelical counterparts appealed to science and philosophy to provide a foundation for faith, those same sources began to undermine the faith they proclaimed. The truth they proclaimed no longer seemed quite so self-evident. One casualty in this appeal to reason and science has been the idea that the Bible is inerrant. For many evangelicals an inerrant Bible was needed if Christians were to have clarity of vision and certainty of faith.

Modernism failed to provide a foundation for faith, but perhaps we have entered a new age, a post-modern age, in which there is less certainty, but more room for faith. In this new era, appeals to biblical inerrancy seem to have lost their value (if ever they had value). Whereas the modernist vision sought to find certainty, something that many persons of faith sought, in this new era there are no certain foundations upon which one can anchor one's faith. So, where do we turn for a Word of God that provides at least some clarity of vision about life and place in the realm of God?[1]

---

1   John Castelein, "Can the Restoration Movement Plea Survive If Belief in Objective Truth is Abandoned?" *Stone-Campbell Journal*, 1 (Spring 1998) 27-44; Philip Kenneson, "Can the Christian Faith Survive if Objective Truth is Abandoned? A Reply to John Castelein," *SCJ*, 2 (Spring 1999) 43-56. On the problem of inerrancy as an effective apologetic see: Jonathan R. Wilson's "Toward a New Evangelical Paradigm of Biblical Authority," *The Nature of Confession: Evangelicals and Postliberals in Conversation*, ed., Timothy R. Phillips and Dennis L. Ockholm, (Downers Grove, IL: IVP, 1996) 151-161. On the change of paradigm as Disciples moved into the postmodern era, see the comments of Paul Blowers in Anthony L. Dunnavant, Richard T. Hughes, Paul Blowers, *Founding Vocation & Future Vision*, (St. Louis: Chalice Press, 1999) 82-83. On Barth's theology, an excellent guide is Gary Dorrien,

Over the past few centuries, both those who challenge the value of the Bible as a source of divine revelation and those who defend it have done so with the tools of the Enlightenment. Both sides of the debate believed they could ascertain the truth – either through historical criticism or through assumptions of historicity. As we take our journey of faith into the twenty-first century, many people both inside and outside the church believe that this earlier paradigm no longer works. If there is no certainty, can we still hope to hear the voice of God in an authoritative way in Scripture? That is, if the historical-critical method of biblical interpretation, which emerged during the modern era undermines claims of infallibility and inerrancy, how do we know when we've heard the divine voice in these texts we call Scripture? That is, for those of us living on the moderate to liberal side of the Christian spectrum, what authority does Scripture have for our lives?

Many years ago, as I struggled with these kinds of questions, I found help in the writings of Karl Barth. It was during seminary, when I took a seminar on Barth's understanding of the Word of God, that I found a way between the Scylla and Charybdis of historical criticism and biblical authority. As I read through the first two volumes of the *Church Dogmatics*, as well as Barth's more accessible *Evangelical Theology*, I discerned a path to a place where I could look to Scripture for a Word from God even though this Word was embedded within very human and culturally bound words.

Of course, turning to Barth for help is not without its difficulties. Many evangelicals look at him as a liberal who jettisoned biblical authority, while many liberals see him as biblical literalist whose views aren't in keeping with modern assumptions. His theology, which emphasizes God's revelation, seems too old hat for the modern age. Nonetheless, Barth's influence, which receded during

---

The Barthian Revolt in Modern Theology: Theology Without Weapons, (Louisville: Westminster John Knox Press, 2000). On the question of the relationship of Scripture to faith, see Henry E. Neufeld, *When People Speak for God.* (Gonzalez, FL: Energion Publications, 2007).

the 1960s and 1970s, seems to be on the ascent of late, especially among those who are called post-liberals and proponents of narrative theology.[2] Whether or not Barth is liberal or conservative, he has been and continues to be a helpful conversation partner of those of us who seek to hear a Word from God in a book that he viewed as both human and divine in origin.

As I have read Barth's discussions of the Word of God, I've found that he tries to put two specific concepts in balance. These concepts include a desire to be faithful hearers of Scripture and the belief that we must approach Scripture not only with reverence but with a critical eye, even making fruitful use of historical-critical tools. Barth never rejected the use of the historical-critical tools he inherited from his liberal teachers, but he believed that they must be put into the service of discerning God's Word revealed in Scripture. For Barth the work of theology and exegesis must be done in service to the proclamation of the Word of God.[3]

---

2   Karl Barth has never been popular in my own denominational circles. Still, while he did not consider himself a Barthian, there are similarities between Barth's approach and that of the British Disciple William Robinson. Robinson noted that a new theology, connected with Barth emerged in the early decades of the century, which affirms the critical interpretation of Scripture and has a new emphasis on the Word of God or Revelation. "It is now seen that the Word of God is an *acted* word much more than a *spoken* word." See Robinson, *Whither Theology?* (London: Lutterworth Press, 1947) 38-39. Though not mentioning Barth, Fred Thompson's article "The Word of God," in *Christian Doctrine*, William J. Richardson, ed., (Cincinnati: Standard Press, 1983) 39-63, also has a Barthian flavor. On the Disciple response to Barth see Stephen V. Sprinkle, *Disciples and Theology: Understanding the Faith of a People in Covenant*, (St. Louis: Chalice Press, 1999) 72-73. Joe Jones, *A Grammar of Christian Faith: Systematic Explorations in Christian Life and Doctrine*, 2 vols. (Lanham, MD: Rowman and Littlefield Publishers, 2002), is an exception to the Disciple tendency to avoid Barth.

3   Angela Dienhart Hancock, *Karl Barth's Emergency Homiletic 1932-1933: A Summons to Prophetic Witness at the Dawn of the Third Reich*, (Grand Rapids: Wm. B. Eerdmans Publishing Co., 2013), p. 198.

How then do we hear God's Word in Scripture, even as we recognize the humanness of the word? Have we allowed Enlightenment understandings of historical and scientific accuracy to inappropriately color the way we hear and understand this Word that comes to us in an ancient document written over a period of many centuries by many different authors? As we seek to engage this Word of God in its human, written form, Barth appears to offer us a non-foundationalist perspective from which we can read Scripture and hear the voice of the divine in the context of this postmodern age.[4] This perspective is one that rests not on philosophical foundations foreign to Scripture but on God's faithfulness to speak through this word called Scripture. Then, as God speaks through this medium, we have a word for today, a word that can serve as an authoritative witness to God's revelation in Jesus Christ.

---

4   Non-foundationalism is a rejection of the ideas espoused by philosophers such as Rene Descartes and Immanuel Kant that one can know the world as it is – that is, have a non-biased understanding of reality. Non-foundationalist philosophers insist that all reality is interpreted from a personal frame of reference. There is no universal or objective form of knowledge available to us. S.V. "Postmodernism," by James K. A. Smith, in *The Cambridge Dictionary of Christian Theology,* Ian A. McFarland, et al., editors. (Cambridge: Cambridge University Press, 2011).

CHAPTER 1

THE WORD OF GOD REVEALED

To understand Karl Barth's doctrine of the Word of God we must start with the Prologue to the Gospel of John; specifically these words: "And the Word became flesh and lived among us, and we have seen his glory, the glory as of a father's only son, full of grace and truth" (Jn 1:14 NRSV).[5] Whatever we say about the nature of the Word of God must begin with the Word become flesh who has dwelt among us in the person of Jesus of Nazareth. That is, we must talk about the person of Jesus Christ as the definitive revelation of God.

For Barth, the Word of God comes to us in three forms, forms that reflect the very nature of the Trinitarian God. In Barth's doctrine of the Word of God, we encounter the Word revealed, the Word written, and the Word proclaimed. All theology or all talk about God, should be based on the presupposition of the Word's threefold nature. But, to say this does not mean that there are three different words of God, any more than to affirm the Trinity is to affirm a belief in three separate gods.[6]

Although there is one Word of God, this Word of God is revealed first and foremost in and through the person of Jesus Christ, who has precedence over the Word written and the Word proclaimed. The written Word and the proclaimed Word depend on God's revelation in Jesus Christ for their existence as Word of God. That is, the written and the proclaimed word, become God's Word

---

5   Karl Barth, *Church Dogmatics*, I/1, 2nd ed., trans. by Geoffrey Bromiley, ed. by Geoffrey Bromiley and T. F. Torrance, (Edinburgh: T&T. Clark, 1975) 119.

6   Barth, *CD*, I/1, 120.

because the God revealed in Jesus Christ speaks through them. In this way, Barth speaks of revelation as that which "engendered Scripture."[7]

Holy Scripture exists as the attestation to the divine self-revelation of God in Christ. Barth emphasizes God's transcendence, and therefore it is in Christ that God broke into human history. While Barth doesn't insist that everything written in the Gospels about Jesus is historic, he does believe that the advent of Christ is an event in history. Barth wrote: "It has happened as a completed event, a fulfilled time, in the sense of the incomplete and changeable and self-changing."[8]

The idea that God's revelation in Christ is a dynamic event in history profoundly influenced Barth's view of Scripture as the written Word of God. By starting with the revelation in Jesus Christ, Barth found it necessary to discard the idea that Scripture is Word of God apart from Christ and the Holy Spirit. Scripture witnesses to or attests God's revelation in Christ, who is the Word of God pure and simple. Yet it is in these very words of Scripture that the "eternal Word" is found. For Barth, when Scripture is understood in this way, we are free to call Scripture God's revelation. This revelation then "establishes the Church and makes its proclamation necessary and possible."[9]

In Barth's Christocentric view of revelation, a view that assumes that Christ is the full and final self-revelation of God, Scripture continually becomes the Word of God because God freely speaks through its words through the agency of the Holy Spirit. It is important to remember that for Barth, God is always the subject of revelation. Therefore, Scripture doesn't become the Word of God, as some have mistakenly thought, when human recipients receive

---

7   Barth, *CD*, I/1, 115.

8   Barth, *CD*, I/1:115-16. See also Karl Barth, Dogmatics in Outline. Harper Torchbooks, (New York: Harper & Row Publishers, 1959), pp. 68-69.

9   Barth, *CD*, I/1:117.

it by faith. Scripture becomes God's word, when God sovereignly acts upon it.[10]

By asserting that God is the subject of revelation rather than human beings, Barth undermines the charge that he is somehow a relativist. God is, for Barth, transcendent and unknowable to sinners (and we're all sinners), but God can sovereignly choose to reveal God's self to humanity. That is, God is the one who initiates contact with humanity in and through Scripture. Confident about God's sovereignty and ability to reveal Godself as God chooses, Barth differentiates between revelation and its witnesses. All that these witnesses, including Scripture and the church's proclamation, can do is "attest and proclaim it."[11] This need not take away from Scripture's authority because God can and does speak in and through it.

As one might expect, John 1:14 stands at the center of Barth's doctrine of revelation: "the Word became flesh and dwelt among us" (NRSV). God's decision to become flesh and dwell among us is good news to the human race. Therefore, Scripture and Christian preaching, if it is rooted in the biblical text, attests to this good news. Again we see the Christocentric nature of Barth's doctrine of revelation. It is also here that we see the unity of the three forms of the Word of God.

The relationship of these three forms of the Word of God are best understood in light of the doctrine of perichoresis. That is, even as the three persons of the Trinity mutually indwell each other, forming a divine unity, so also do these three forms of the Word God find unity through a the mutual indwelling.[12] This unity of the three forms of the Word stands as the guarantee against subjectivism. The reader of Scripture and the preacher of the good news do not control the Word. The reader and the preacher receive this Word of God as God's chosen witness to God's self-revelation.

10 Barth, *CD*, I/1:117.
11 Barth, *CD*, I/1: 120.
12 Geoffrey W. Bromiley, *Introduction to the Theology of Karl Barth*, (Grand Rapids: Wm. B. Eerdmans Publishing Co., 1979), p. 8.

To say that God is knowable, is not to say that God is provable, or discerned outside of God's own decision to be known. Barth writes in his *Dogmatics in Outline:*

> No attempt is made in the Bible to define God – that is, to grasp God in our concepts. In the Bible God's name is named, not as philosophers do it, as the name of a timeless Being, surpassing the world, alien and supreme, but as the name of the living, acting, working Subject who makes Himself known. The Bible tells the story of God; it narrates His deeds and the history of this God in the highest, as it takes place on earth in the human sphere.[13]

For those engaged in proclaiming the Gospel, then it is important to remember that this proclamation is rooted in God's own story.

The security that we seem to desire as we pursue our faith journey will not be provided by an objective revelation that can be found printed on the pages of a book. We can't hope to demonstrate beyond the shadow of doubt the truth of our confession. Instead, we must start where God begins, with God's revelation, which is found revealed in the person of Jesus Christ, the one in whom the transcendent God has chosen to be revealed. It is to this event in salvation history that Scripture provides an authoritative witness for believers of every age.

---

13 Barth, *Dogmatics in Outline*, p. 38.

CHAPTER 2

THE WITNESS TO REVELATION

Scripture is an authoritative witness to God's revelation in Jesus Christ. Karl Barth consciously chose to define Scripture as witness rather than as revelation. By doing this, Barth tried to preserve the dynamic and personal nature of revelation. For him, God is transcendent and can only be known when God chooses to be revealed. Scripture becomes this witness when it points beyond itself to God, who is the ultimate authority. [14]

Although Scripture gives its witness to God's revelation that lies beyond the written word, it is in these words, written by humans who were called by God to proclaim the good news, that we encounter God's Word for us. God guarantees the truthfulness of this by fulfilling it. As such, "the Word of God is the criterion of the church, Church proclamation, and dogmatics. When we ask where the possibility of knowledge of God's Word is to be sought, we are asking where the criterion is to be sought with which dogmatics works."[15]

The idea that Scripture is a witness to God's revelation and not revelation in and of itself places a limitation on Scripture. It means that Scripture, as witness to revelation, is not self-sufficient. Instead, it depends on something or someone else lying beyond the written word for God's presence and purpose to be revealed. Barth makes it clear that a "witness is not absolutely identical with that to which it witnesses." Therefore, "in the Bible we meet with human

---

14 Barth, *CD*, I/2, trans. by G. T. Thomson and Harold Knight; ed. by Geoffrey Bromiley and T. F. Torrance, (Edinburgh: T. & T. Clark, 1956), p. 458.
15 Barth, *CD*, I/1: 212-214.

words written in human speech, and in these words, and therefore by means of them, we hear of the lordship of the triune God."[16]

Since Scripture is not "absolutely identical" to God's revelation then humans cannot have access to a univocal knowledge of God. For Barth, human language and intellect by its very nature is inadequate to obtaining complete knowledge of God. Although some would argue that human language is adequate to this task, Barth would not put this kind of confidence in human reason. He believed that sin distorted human knowledge of God, making all knowledge of God dependent on God's decision to be known. For Barth, human knowledge of God comes indirectly by way of analogy. We perceive this analogy through faith, as a gift of God. Although the idea of an analogy implies a similarity between an object and the means of conveyance, the dissimilarity prevents us from speaking infallibly about God. We can have knowledge of God, but it will be imperfect, because God presents "himself as their true object."[17]

The truth of Barth's position becomes apparent when we look at the way in which Scripture speaks of God. If we speak univocally about God, then we must affirm God's maleness. If God is a literal father, then we might conclude that God has children in the same way as human parents. This is, after all, the interpretation of God's fatherhood taken by Joseph Smith and the Church of Jesus Christ of Latter Day Saints. This position becomes untenable, however, if we understand God to be neither male nor female (or beyond gender).

---

16 Barth, *CD*, I/2, 463.

17 Karl Barth, *God in Action*, (Manhasset, NY: Round Table Press, 1963), p. 11. Donald Bloesch, A Theology of Word and Spirit: Authority and Method in Theology, (Downers Grove: InterVarsity Press, 1992) 68-69. Bromiley, Introduction, 67. See Ronald Nash, The Word of God and the Mind of Man, (Grand Rapids: Zondervan Publishing Co., 1982) 68-69, for a good example of an affirmation of the adequacy of human language to convey God's thoughts.

The dissimilarity between the subject of revelation and its recipients forced Barth to reject the doctrine of inerrancy as untenable. Although Barth was unclear about what constitutes an error, his use of the historical-critical method made it difficult for him to affirm the existence of an error-free text. All that he would say is that since Scripture is a human witness it has a "capacity for error." Yet, even if Scripture has this capacity, we must "face the objection and believe" that God is revealed to us in Scripture.[18] As Bernard Ramm points out, "Barth has the linguists on his side when he says no such perfection in language can be achieved."[19] If Scripture has this capacity, then it would seem appropriate to argue with Scripture when its witness becomes distorted by its cultural context.

The idea of infallibility falters in the face of modern science as well. If nothing else, science requires that we reject a literalist reading of the creation stories found in the biblical text. That doesn't mean they do not convey truth, it simply means they do not provide scientific facts. The issue is not whether Scripture is wrong about science or history, but whether we should see Scripture as a scientific/historical text.

Although Barth speaks of the Bible as history, he doesn't envision the modern practice of academic history. Rather this is a history that is theological in orientation. Scripture tells a story about how God has made' Godself known to humanity within history. Scripture, therefore, must be judged on this basis and not on foreign criteria. We are mistaken if we insist that the Bible should offer specific information that corresponds to modern scientific findings. The human authors of Scripture lived in a particular time and place and their words and understandings reflect the historical and scientific understandings of that time.

---

18 Barth, *CD*, I/2: 508-9.

19 Bernard Ramm, *After Fundamentalism*, (San Francisco: Harper and Row, 1983), 90.

We cannot expect or demand a compendium of solomonic or even divine knowledge of all things in heaven and earth, natural, historical, and human, to be mediated to the prophets and the apostles in and with their encounter with divine revelation, possessing which they have to be differentiated not only from their own, but from every age as the bearers and representatives of an ideal culture and therefore as the inerrant proclaimers of all and every truth.[20]

That God chose to become known to us in a specific time and place does not baptize that era or make that culture or even its church order paradigmatic for all ages to come. There was no Golden Age for the church, as some Restorationists[21] would have us believe. Indeed, Greek, Hebrew, and Aramaic do not convey God's revelation because they are better or holier than other languages. These simply were the languages spoken at the time the words of Scripture was put down on paper. Other languages could just as easily have been chosen, just as God could have chosen other times and places to be revealed to us. Despite this truth, we must still attend to the original languages and cultures, for it is in these contexts that God chose to become known to us. If we are to hear God's Word in Scripture then we must understand the contexts in which the words we encounter in Scripture were written without making these contexts normative.

Scripture's capacity for error doesn't prevent it from serving as a normative witness to Christ.

We believe that Scripture is the Word of God. But when we say that we say more than we can say in view of our own

---

20 Barth, *CD*, I/2: 508.

21 There have been a variety of Restorationist movements, many of which envision a golden age that should be replicated in the modern period. Restorationists often point to the Book of Acts, seeing in it a blue print for the modern church. Such a vision is foreign to Barth's understanding.

present: in recollection and expectation we look to the present of an event that God alone can cause.[22]

Barth had supreme confidence in God's ability to be heard; therefore he was untroubled with the thought that we encounter the Word of God in and through fallible human words provided to us by prophets and apostles. Although God's Word comes to us in human words, words we must take seriously by studying them and expounding them according to their historical meaning, we can still find God's Word to us in these very human words. That is because these human words point beyond themselves to "a fact, an object."[23]

Scripture as witness also is conditional in nature, for the Word of God comes to us through the agency of human mediators, whether these mediators are the various authors of Scripture or the expositors and preachers of this Word. Therefore, Barth found it helpful to speak of Scripture and proclamation becoming the Word of God. He wrote that "if the Word of God is God himself even in Holy Scripture and Church Proclamation, it is because this is so in the revelation to which they bear witness."[24] It is God who makes the human witness the Word of God, and the conditional nature of this witness results from its dependence on God's act of revelation. It is this Word of God that is the highest court of appeal, for this revelation is none other than God.[25] This does not mean that he denies that Scripture has authority, but it is not the final authority. The one who is the ultimate authority is the one who stands behind Scripture and speaks through it. To think otherwise entices us to us to make Scripture an idol, that is, a god.

Barth conceives of the Word of God being an act or event in history that is mediated to us through the testimony of Scripture. Because we are material beings, we receive this witness in material

---

22 Barth, *CD*, I/2: 512.
23 Barth, *CD*, I/2:464.
24 Barth, *CD*, I/1, 304.
25 Barth, *CD*, I/1, 305.

form. While the Word of God is spiritual in nature, because we are natural beings, we can't receive this Word outside the material. Therefore, we receive this Word through Scripture, Proclamation, and the Sacraments.[26]

Although the Word of God is a spiritual event that does not mean that it is irrational or non-cognitive. The very existence of Scripture is a reminder that God has chosen to be revealed in and through human rationality. But, revelation is more than simply a rational or philosophical construct. It is not, therefore, something that humans can control.

> God's Word is not a thing to be described nor a term to be defined. It is neither a matter nor an idea. It is not "a truth" not even the highest truth. It is **the** truth as it is God's speaking person, *dei loque tis persona*.[27]

Abstracting the Word of God from the person of God is not possible, because Scripture is always in the process of becoming the Word of God. That is, it becomes the Word of God when God chooses to be present in it. This means that we misuse Scripture when we conceive of it being the source of abstract propositional truth that we can organize and systematize. We also misuse it when we turn it into a moral rule book or a theological handbook. When we do this, it ceases to be the Word of God that bears witness to the one whom most fully reveals God – the Word made flesh (John 1:14).

Although Barth doesn't reject the idea that we can make rational statements about God or that Scripture makes rational statements, he does reject the idea that we can find propositional forms of revelation in Scripture. Indeed, the very idea of propositional revelation is a very modern concept. It is an Enlightenment practice to systematize and catalogue revelation in such a way that we can find in it specific answers to every question under the sun.

---

26 Barth, *CD*, I/1, 133-34.
27 Barth, *CD*, I/1, 136.

Indeed, such an idea owes more to Francis Bacon than to the biblical authors.

Barth did not conceive of Scripture serving as a compendium of propositions about God or anything else. Propositions speak about something but they can't become revelational, because revelation is personal and dynamic. Propositions on the other hand, by their nature, are abstract and static.[28] If we see the Word and the Son as equivalent it is, Barth believed, impossible to "say anything doctrinaire in understanding the Word of God."[29] This means that a barrier has been set up against conceiving of a "fixed sum of revealed propositions which can be systematized like the sections of a corpus of law. The only system in Holy Scripture . . . is revelation, i.e., Jesus Christ."[30]

Barth may have rejected the idea of propositional revelation, but he did believe that God reveals Godself through statements and words, including the words of the prophets and the apostles. We can receive the Word of God in the words of Scripture, but revelation remains spiritual in nature. Revelation isn't irrational, but it can't be objectified or accessed directly. God remains a free subject and God's Word continues to be under God's control, not ours.[31] Therefore, you can't write a system of propositions and have full and complete understanding of God.

Barth made a strong case for the personal nature of revelation, but he didn't see this as a "deverbalizing" of the Word of God. Revelation is communicated through Scripture, but we must always remember that it is a mediated word. Therefore, it is better to say – "the Bible reads" rather than "the Bible says."

Since God has sovereignty over Scripture, God has "free control over the wording of Scripture" and can use it to convey revelation in whatever way God sees fit. This means that God has erected a wall to prevent the recipients of the Word from "reducing

28   Barth, *CD*, I/1, 137.
29   Barth, *CD*, I/1, 137.
30   Barth, *CD*, I/1, 137.
31   Barth, *CD*, I/1, 138-39.

its wording to a human system or using its wording to establish and construct a human system."[32]

Barth rejected any system that tried to reduce Scripture to a set of propositions that humans can control. He emphatically insisted that the Word of God should be allowed the freedom to speak for itself. Therefore, he responded coldly to seventeenth-century Protestant theological positions because they tried to control the text of Scripture by systematizing it. In doing this, these theologians diminished the faith to the point where all necessary aspects of the Christian religion were contained in this book, completely abrogating God's freedom and making it unnecessary for God to speak to us through the text.

The words of Scripture may be inspired by God, but this inspiration, according to Barth, isn't intrinsic to the Bible as a book. Inspiration, for Barth, is a continual process, with God as the subject of inspiration. To accept the idea of permanent inspiration freezes the "relationship between Scripture and revelation.[33] While the Holy Spirit led the authors of Scripture in their recording of the witness to God's self-revelation in Jesus Christ, the doctrine of inspiration does not end there. Inspiration could also include the illumination of the person who comes to Scripture in faith to receive the Word of God, making inspiration a continuing event dependent on the Holy Spirit. This broader understanding of inspiration led Barth to view inerrancy as a hardening of inspiration and a "secular postulate." The secularity of this doctrine was derived from the assumption that humans could decide what was authoritative.

The secular nature of this postulate showed itself plainly in the assumption that we may freely reproach the good God if it is not fulfilled, threatening him with distrust, skepticism and atheism — a threat which was no less freely carried out in

---

32 Barth, *CD*, I/1, 139.
33 Barth, *CD*, I/1, 124.

the following generations, when men became convinced that the postulate could not be fulfilled.[34]

That is, one can set up a false basis of security that will ultimately fail, producing a crisis of faith. This occurs because many believers place their confidence in the Bible rather than in God's ability to speak for Godself. In so doing, they create for themselves a "paper Pope," which, unlike the Roman Pope, it was "wholly given up into the hands of its interpreters. It was no longer a free and spiritual force, but an instrument of human power."[35] For Barth, inspiration was God's sovereign control of this witness to divine revelation.

In defining inspiration, Barth made eight fundamental points. First, the Word of God is a "being and event which are not under human control." Second, Word of God is not a state or fact, but an event relevant to us, "an event which is an act of God, an act of God which rests on a free decision." Third, the Word is a "miracle of God." Fourth, the miraculous nature of the Word does not compromise its human form as Scripture. Fifth, inspiration does not mean that the Word is inherent to Scripture permanently. Sixth, God decides "when, where, and how the Bible shows itself to us in this event as the Word of God." Seventh, there is a twofold sense to inspiration: on one hand there is the text and what it reports that God said; on the other hand, verbal inspiration does not mean the Bible is infallible. Instead it means that the "fallible and faulty human word is as such used by God and has to be received and heard in spite of its human fallibility." Finally, we cannot reduce inspiration to our faith in it, "even though we understand this faith as the gift and work of God in us."[36] God speaks through the witness of Scripture but we do not place our faith in this witness but in the God who speaks through it.

---

34 Barth, *CD*, I/2, 525.
35 Barth, *CD*, I/2, 525-26.
36 Barth, *CD*, I/2, 527-34.

As a fully human word, the words of Scripture are conditioned by their cultural context and by the inadequacies of human language to convey truth perfectly. Yet, according to Barth, this fallible human word is also the unique Word of God. Though Barth distinguishes between Scripture and Word of God, he does not teach that Scripture is one witness among many. Neither oral tradition nor human experience has the same level of authority as Scripture, which stands first as the primary witness to the incarnation, death, and resurrection of Jesus Christ. In Scripture the words of the apostles and prophets bear witness to the good news of Jesus Christ. No other witness has the authority of the God revealed in history. Tradition and experience have a certain kind of authority, but this authority is secondary to that of Scripture, for they are only "expositions of the basic statement that there is a Word of God for the Church: in that it receives in the Bible the witness of divine revelation."[37] Scripture stands as the authoritative Word for the church because it offers the unique witness to God's self-revelation in Jesus Christ.

---

37 Barth, *CD*, I/2, 463. This helps counterbalance the current interest in the Wesleyan quadrilateral of Scripture, reason, experience, and tradition. Wesley would have been much closer to Barth than some of his current advocates who see these four being equivalent witnesses. Experience, Tradition, and Reason are essential, but secondary sources of thinking about the God revealed in Jesus Christ and first and foremost witnessed to by the Word written, i.e. Scripture.

CHAPTER 3

THE AUTHORITATIVE WITNESS TO REVELATION

Jesus came into the world and preached the kingdom of God. This idea of kingdom or realm of God suggests that God has supreme and ultimate authority over church and world. Barth affirmed the sovereignty of God, but he understood that this authority can be mediated through the agency of human witnesses. Prophets and apostles offer us this witness and provide the church the necessary authority to order and govern itself for the purpose of proclaiming the good news of Jesus Christ. Although Scripture is not, according to Barth, inerrant, it is an adequate guide for the church. He was confident that God could speak through these human words and didn't feel the need to distinguish between the human and the divine in Scripture.

Barth forged his doctrine of biblical authority in the midst of what he considered two major errors then facing the church: Roman Catholic adherence to church tradition and Neo-Protestant reliance on human experience. In response, Barth contended that Scripture alone offered an authoritative word to the church. It's important to remember that he took this position in the context of the Nazi threat to the German churches. The German Christian Movement and other Nationalist theologians sought to rethink Christian theology in relationship to the German national experience. In putting forth his understanding of revelation and authority, he sought to affirm God's sovereignty over the church. Scripture provided the Word through which God continued to speak.[38] Barth had reason to fear the appeal to human reason and

---

38 Barth, *CD*, I/2, 574-575. I would recommend reading Angela Dienhart Hancock Karl Barth's Emergency Homiletic 1932-1933 to get a sense of what Barth faced as he developed his theology of the Word.

experience. In his context German nationalism offered what was for many a compelling revisioning of the faith, one that would further the rebirth of nation. In our own context, we can perhaps be more open to human experience being a vehicle for God's Word to be revealed, but Barth's own background is a reminder of the pitfalls.[39]

Why should Scripture be the church's primal authority? It is, Barth declares, the "oldest extant record of the origin and therefore the basis and nature of the church."[40] Simply put, it has authority because of its historic precedence. But, this cannot be the sole basis of its authority. As a historical record, Scripture remains a very human word. For it to serve as a divinely-backed authority it must be rooted in the living and dynamic nature of the Word of God. That is, it becomes authoritative because it is a living Word that is incarnate in the words God has chosen to speak through. In this way revelation can be seen as verbal, but revelation in Barth's understanding transcends human understanding and human language. It is best to say that the Revelation of God – The Word of God – has adapted himself to human words. What is authoritative is not the book itself, but the "voice the men apprehended through the book and letter, and in the voice of these men the voice of Him who called them to speak, which is authority in the Church."[41]

Although Scripture doesn't offer an inerrant record of God's revelation, it does stand over all attempts to do theology. In making this claim, Barth would remind us that tradition, reason, and experience, as helpful as they may be, stand under the judgment of Scripture. Therefore, theologians cannot claim either superiority or equality with this record. One finds Scripture speaking authoritatively even in the "smallest, strangest, simplest, or obscurest among the Biblical witnesses," who have "an incomparable

---

39 For a helpful attempt to keep scripture and experience in proper balance, see Luke Timothy Johnson's *Scripture and Discernment: Decision Making in the Church*, (Nashville: Abingdon Press, 1996).
40 Barth, *CD*, I/2, 540.
41 Barth, *CD*, I/2, 581.

advantage over even the most pious scholarly, and sagacious latter day theologian."[42]

Scripture has authority for us because God chose it above all other possible records and words to speak through. However, because it brings to us God's word doesn't mean that it speaks authoritatively to all fields of endeavor.

> The post-biblical theologian may, no doubt, possess a better astronomy, geography, zoology, psychology, physiology, and so on than these biblical witnesses possessed; but as for the Word of God, he is not justified in comporting himself in relationship to those witnesses as though he knew more about the Word than they.[43]

Genesis 1 and 2 might speak differently than the modern scientist, but this doesn't mean Genesis cannot be a vehicle of God's revelation. Even if the words of Genesis 1-2 reflected how the authors envisioned the world, they were not doing science. What we find here is saga, which is different from myth. In the *Dogmatics in Outline* we read:

> The Bible speaks in Genesis 1 and 2 of events which lie outside of our historical knowledge. But it speaks upon the basis of knowledge, which is related to history. In fact, the wonderful thing about the biblical creation narratives is that they stand in strict connection with the history of Israel, and so with the story of God's action in the covenant with man.[44]

We should not expect to find a modern scientific account of the origins of the earth, but we will find an explication of God's efforts at covenanting with humanity.

---

42 Karl Barth, *Evangelical Theology: An Introduction*, trans., Grover Foley, (Grand Rapids: Wm. B. Eerdmans, 1963) 31-32.

43 Barth, *Evangelical Theology*, 31.

44 Karl Barth, *Dogmatics in Outline*, (New York: Harper & Row, Publishers, 1959), p. 51.

Acceptance of biblical authority is demonstrated not in apologetics or polemics, but in our obedience to it as God's Word. It is important to confess the authority of Scripture, but to confess its authority and then not live one's life according to this word is simply untenable. Barth wrote that "the existence of the Church of Jesus Christ stands or falls with the fact that it obeys as the apostles and prophets obeyed their Lord."[45]

Confession of Scripture's authority isn't just a private matter; it is a public event that takes place in the confines of the church that stands under the authority of Scripture. The interplay of Scripture and church is seen in the formation of the canon, a process that doesn't determine authority but recognizes it, for the Bible witnesses to its own canonicity. Scripture's power to speak with divine authority protected it from the inroads of human self-will that have tried to control it.[46] Though there is a place for creeds, confessions, the Fathers, and human experience, these authorities take their place underneath Scripture.

---

45 Barth, *CD*, I/2, 543.
46 Barth, *CD*, I/2, 598.

Conclusion

One needn't accept Barthianism as a system to appreciate his desire to hear and apply Scripture as a Word from God to the contemporary world. It is, in fact, his willingness to let Scripture speak for itself that makes his witness most helpful in our own day. At a time when the broader culture is questioning the philosophical foundations upon which the Enlightenment project was built, thereby freeing us from our previous philosophical anchorage, Barth calls us to listen to Scripture in a Christocentric fashion. That is, he calls us to read Scripture in light of the person and ministry of Jesus. If we do this then we will have the opportunity to hear a Word from God that speaks to our day.

The solution to the problem of religious authority cannot be found in making the Bible an infallible source of divine authority. But, even if we cannot turn to it for an infallible word, we can hear in these texts we call Scripture the voice of God. Without the framework of inerrancy, this might be a more difficult task, but it's not impossible. What is required of us is trust that God is able and willing to speak to us. In this postmodern age, we will be unable to offer a fool proof apologetic for God or Scripture. We can't gather together our evidence demanding a verdict and sit on this foundation and expect the world to come and join us. Instead, we must allow the Spirit of God to attest the message of this Word. Although experience is not the primary authority in the church, human experience allows us to ask questions of Scripture so that will allow God to speak a word of wisdom and grace to us. Indeed, even if the canon itself is closed, that doesn't mean God has ceased to speak. Surely, God is not mute and can offer a new word that speaks to our own age, even if it is to be found within an ancient word.

Consider that over time many have recognized that the way Scripture speaks of women or slavery cannot be seen as reflecting

God's vision. I believe that we are seeing the same thing occur today with regard to gay, lesbian, bisexual, transgender, persons. Our experiences are forcing us to ask new questions of Scripture, and many of us are hearing a new word from God.

Barth accepted the Bible as it stood before him. He didn't find it necessary to harmonize difficult passages or appeal to non-extant original autographs. He made no excuses for the text, nor was he embarrassed by its humanness. Even in its humanness, Scripture served for him as God's authoritative Word, for God continues to speak through its pages. As Disciples of Christ theologian William Robinson put it many years ago as he was engaging with Barth's theology: "The Bible tells the story of God's bid for fellowship with man, who through sin has broken fellowship with God."[47] Even a critical reading of the text of scripture cannot keep it from fulfilling this purpose, for Scripture tells the story of the mighty acts of God, and it is this God and not we who control its usefulness.

One of the benefits of Barth's threefold understanding of the Word of God is that it allows us to envision the work of preaching as part of this vision. When rooted in the biblical witness to Jesus Christ, the proclamation of the church becomes a Word of God – a witness to God's presence and action in the world. The testimony of human witnesses comes into service of the Word of God, as God chooses to speak through these words. It isn't a special quality of the person that gives evidence of this witness, but rather "it rests wholly and exclusively in that God, in his law suit against men, chooses these men in particular, and makes disciples, apostles, and prophets to serve Him as His witnesses in His cause."[48]

As a personal word, I must confess that my encounter with Barth's threefold understanding of the Word of God helped me to overcome my fundamentalist fear that if this text wasn't inerrant,

47 Robinson, *Whither Theology? Some Essential Biblical Patterns*, (London: Lutterworth Press, 1947), p. 47.
48 Karl Barth, *God In Action*, Introduction by Elmer G. Homrighausen, translated by E. G. Homrighausen and Karl J. Ernst, (Manhasset, NY: Round Table Press, 1963), p. 97.

that it's word on science was the final word, or that it's word on the role of women was the final word, then I would have to retreat from the world as it is. My own engagement with science and culture raised questions about how to interpret this text that lay before me. Barth provided me a path forward. His vision of the Word of God allowed me to make use of critical tools of interpretation and also hear God's revelation anew in the text of Scripture. Perhaps he can do this for others who struggle to keep in proper balance the need to interpret and apply Scripture even as they read it as a normative Word.

TOPICAL LINE DRIVES

Straight to the Point in under 44 Pages

All Topical Line Drives volumes are priced at $4.99 print and 99¢ in all ebook formats.

Available

The Authorship of Hebrews: The Case for Paul	David Alan Black
What Protestants Need to Know about Roman Catholics	Robert LaRochelle
What Roman Catholics Need to Know about Protestants	Robert LaRochelle
Forgiveness: Finding Freedom from Your Past	Harvey Brown, Jr.
Process Theology: Embracing Adventure with God	Bruce Epperly
Holistic Spirituality: Life Transforming Wisdom from the Letter of James	Bruce Epperly
To Date or Not to Date: What the Bible Says about Pre-Marital Relationships	D. Kevin Brown
The Eucharist: Encounters with Jesus at the Table	Robert D. Cornwall
The Authority of Scripture in a Postmodern Age: Some Help from Karl Barth	Robert D. Cornwall
Rendering unto Caesar	Chris Surber
The Caregiver's Beattitudes	Robert Martin
What is Wrong with Social Justice	Elgin Hushbeck, Jr.

Forthcoming

God the Creator: The Variety of Christian Views on Origins	Henry Neufeld
I'm Right and You're Wrong	Steve Kindle
Stewardship: It's More than Money	Steve Kindle
Why Christians Should Care about Their Jewish Roots	Nancy Petrey
A Cup of Cold Water	Chris Surber
Words of Woe: Alternative Lectionary Texts	Robert D. Cornwall

Planned

Christian Existentialism	David Moffett-Moore
Paths to Prayer	David Moffett-Moore

(The titles of planned volumes may change before release.)

Generous Quantity Discounts Available
Dealer Inquiries Welcome
Energion Publications — P.O. Box 841
Gonzalez, FL 32560
Website: http://energionpubs.com
Phone: (850) 525-3916

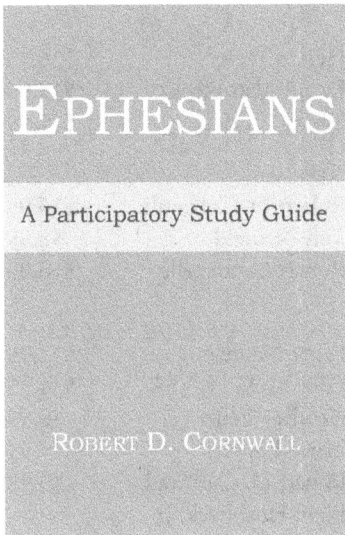

EPHESIANS

A Participatory Study Guide

ROBERT D. CORNWALL

Bob Cornwall combines the mind of a scholar and the heart of a pastor in this participatory study guide on Ephesians.

Dr. Glen Miles
Senior Minister
Country Club Christian Church
(Disciples of Christ)
Kansas City, MO

BY ROBERT D. CORNWALL

The time is now for mainline churches to reappropriate the full spectrum of the spiritual gifts for their contemporary tasks.

Amos Yong, Ph.D.
Dean
Divinity School
Regent University
Author of *Spirit of Love*

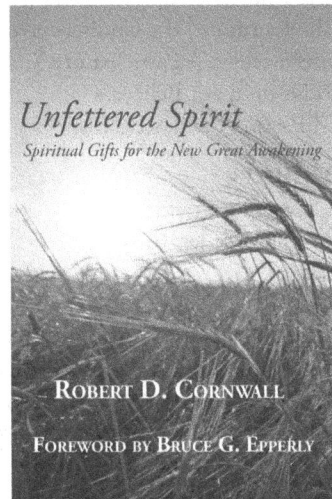

Unfettered Spirit
Spiritual Gifts for the New Great Awakening

ROBERT D. CORNWALL

FOREWORD BY BRUCE G. EPPERLY

MORE FROM ENERGION PUBLICATIONS

Personal Study

Finding My Way in Christianity	Herold Weiss	$16.99
The Jesus Paradigm	David Alan Black	$17.99
When People Speak for God	Henry Neufeld	$17.99

Christian Living

Faith in the Public Square	Robert D. Cornwall	$16.99
Grief: Finding the Candle of Light	Jody Neufeld	$8.99
Crossing the Street	Robert LaRochelle	$16.99

Bible Study

Learning and Living Scripture	Lentz/Neufeld	$12.99
From Inspiration to Understanding	Edward W. H. Vick	$24.99
Luke: A Participatory Study Guide	Geoffrey Lentz	$8.99
Philippians: A Participatory Study Guide	Bruce Epperly	$9.99
Ephesians: A Participatory Study Guide	Robert D. Cornwall	$9.99
Evidence for the Bible	Elgin Hushbeck, Jr.	

Theology

Creation in Scripture	Herold Weiss	$12.99
Creation: the Christian Doctrine	Edward W. H. Vick	$12.99
Ultimate Allegiance	Robert D. Cornwall	$9.99
History and Christian Faith	Edward W. H. Vick	$9.99
The Church Under the Cross	William Powell Tuck	$11.99
The Journey to the Undiscovered Country	William Powell Tuck	$9.99
Eschatology: A Participatory Study Guide	Edward W. H. Vick	$9.99
Philosophy for Believers	Edward W. H. Vick	$14.99
Christianity and Secularism	Elgin Hushbeck, Jr.	$16.99

Ministry

Clergy Table Talk	Kent Ira Groff	$9.99
So Much Older Then …	Robert LaRochelle	$9.99

Generous Quantity Discounts Available
Dealer Inquiries Welcome
Energion Publications — P.O. Box 841
Gonzalez, FL 32560
Website: http://energionpubs.com
Phone: (850) 525-3916

www.ingramcontent.com/pod-product-compliance
Lightning Source LLC
Chambersburg PA
CBHW011751020426
42331CB00014B/3351